CHASIN' CRUSTACEANS
Stories Behind the Names of Maine Lobster Boats

VICTOR COLE

Down East Books

Down East Books

Published by Down East Books
A wholly owned subsidiary of The Rowman & Littlefield Publishing Group, Inc.
4501 Forbes Boulevard, Suite 200, Lanham, Maryland 20706
www.rowman.com

Unit A, Whitacre Mews, 26-34 Stannary Street, London SE11 4AB

Distributed by NATIONAL BOOK NETWORK

Library of Congress Cataloging in Publication data available

ISBN 978-1-60893-448-5 (cloth : alk. paper) — ISBN 978-1-60893-449-2 (electronic)

The paper used in this publication meets the minimum requirements of American National Standard for Information Sciences—Permanence of Paper for Printed Library Materials, ANSI/NISO Z39.48-1992.

*T*here is pride in a name, and it runs deep. To many lobstermen, naming our boat is similar to naming a child. Our lobster boats are our lifeline. We literally depend on their safe condition, their seaworthiness, and their good fortune to keep us alive. We spend a great deal of time aboard this vessel, and sometimes in extreme conditions. When we call each other on the VHF radio we use boat names:

"Killing Time . . . this is Blue-By-U . . . you on this channel?"

Federally documented boats are required to be named. This is our identifying feature to the U.S. Coast Guard, the Maine Marine Patrol, and our fellow fishermen.

Without a love for our boats that we named with our heart the trust, partnership, and confidence would not be there.

There are over six thousand licensed lobstermen in Maine. The stories in this book tell the tales of what influenced their choice of a boat name. Many reflect love and appreciation for their loved ones. Others refer to an event that is so important in their lives that they want to keep it alive. Some are just downright funny.

The lobster boat names and the stories behind them are a glimpse into the lives of Maine lobster harvesters. It has been a great experience for me to meet many of my fellow lobstermen featured in this book and to learn their heartfelt stories. I hope you enjoy them as well.

— Victor Cole
Tenants Harbor

Long Tail Duck

Victor Cole
Port Clyde

"Squaw" is considered to be a derogatory name for women and was offensive to the Indian nation. Because of this, the names of hundreds of locations, from mountains to parks, were changed.

The state of Maine changed the name of the beautiful migratory duck, old squaw, to long tail duck. This change occurred at the time I was naming my boat and I figured I might have the only *Long Tail Duck* out there.

My previous boat, which I used for lobstering, as well as getting to an island that my wife and I caretake, was a fairly old wooden boat. She took a lot of care to keep her in shape. I named her *Caretaker*—seemed appropriate given the double meaning.

16th Avenue

Wendall and Donna Bryant
Cutler

I named my boat after the song "16th Avenue," sung by Lacy Dalton. The song is about a dream come true, and that is what our boat is.

Tide-N-Half

Tommy Bridges
Corea

My nickname is Tommy Tide and my son, Bryan Bridges, is nicknamed Half Tide, so we named our boat *Tide-N-Half*!

51

William R. (Billy Bob) Faulkinham
Winter Harbor

The name of my boat is *51*. When people see it they are usually puzzled. It's too short to be a registration number and too odd to be a name. I've been asked over a hundred times what it means. I've even been asked if it stands for 151 rum—the answer is no. Fifteen years ago when I was naming my first big boat I decided on a name that was very meaningful and close to my heart.

I was a senior in high school in 1996, and my cousin Adam was a junior. In the summer of that year Adam was taken from us in a tragic car accident. He was seventeen. We were very close and spent a lot of time playing basketball. Adam's uniform number was 51. I couldn't name my boat anything else.

In 2005, when I launched my new boat, I proudly named her *51*, too. I don't know if I'll ever have another new boat, but if I do it will be named *51*.

This number holds a lot of significance for me and has

always brought me luck. When I purchased my first home I didn't even know it, but the address ended up being 51 Walters Road. It was the only house on the road. My wife and I got married on 5/1, 2010. And the last two digits of my son's social security number are 51.

***

Ronda Lynn

Winston (Rudy) Pease
Port Clyde

The last boat that I owned was the *Ronda Lynn*, named after my youngest daughter. Ronda was 7 years old when she christened it at the Port Clyde public landing in 1983.

A-Salt-Weapon

Mike Ausplund
Tenants Harbor

When a guy thinks something is cool and it's a machine, they often describe it as "a weapon." Being on the ocean, my boat is *A-Salt Weapon*. No guns on board.

Trigger

Leroy Rogers
Owls Head

My husband fishes out of Ship N Shore Wharf in Owls Head and he's owned a couple of other boats before this one. After years of nagging I finally got him to name this one *Trigger* because his name is Leroy Rogers and everyone has always called him Roy.

Abenaki and *Helvetia*

Anson Norton
Crie Haven

There have been two boats named *Helvetia* in my family. The first was a three-masted schooner of my great grandfather's that was lost at sea off Cape Hatteras. The second *Helvetia* was mine. It was a 35-foot boat built at Clark Island Boat Yard and lost in a fire at the boatyard in March of 2000.

When I had the next boat built I changed the name to *Abenaki*. Two *Helvetia*s were enough for me. I think someone was trying to tell me something. *Abenaki* means "people of the dawn;" they were the native people of the Northeast. The *Abenaki* is now thirteen years old and going strong thanks to Dan at Clark Island Boat Yard.

Acts 2:38

Richard V. Eaton
Brooklin

I actually paid for my husband's boat with a small inheritance from my mother's passing, so I got to name it. Since "Acts 2:38" is a key scripture in the Bible that tells how you get saved, I wanted to put it out there so people would see it and maybe look it up.

— Robbie Eaton

Mamiluem

Walter Lucas
Cundy's Harbor

This name comes from the first two letters of each of my grandchildren's middle names, in the order they were born.

Anxiety

Heron Arey
Millbridge

I like names that aren't the normal wife, daughter, son, etc. One word names are favorites, too. It took me a long time to come up with the perfect one for my liking. When my wife and I thought it up we realized what better name than *Anxiety* for a boat.

Lobster fishing is full of anxiety. You never know if there will be lobsters, how much they will be worth, if the boat is going to run perfect, or if something will go wrong. Along with many other things.

This is my first boat. I have been a stern man for fifteen years and I'm running this boat on my days off and after work. I am working toward going as my own captain. It's not a big boat, but it's getting the job done.

Brother Pidge

Inez E. Frazier
Great Wass Island

I am a lobster fisherwoman. My boat's name is *Brother Pidge*. In 1972, when I was 12 and my brother, Alvin "Pidge" Beal, was 17, he and my father had a boating accident. My brother saved my father, John Beal, Sr. and lost his own life. He has always been a hero. He was loved by all who knew him. I wanted to keep his memory alive and therefore, I named my boat for him. My mother, sister, and I recently received, on his behalf, the Certificate of Valor for his efforts on that day.

This is the story of the tragic day Alvin "Pidge" Beal drowned in the waters off Great Wass Island. The nightmare started with Margaret, our mother, having a dream of him drowning the night before the fateful day. She begged her husband John, who went to haul with him to stay home. John prevailed, stating, "We can't keep the boy captive . . . that was only a dream."

The two went off to haul in their 16-foot outboard. They had just hauled their last trap and were getting ready to head home when a tall wave came from out of nowhere. The wave flipped the boat, tossing both into the frigid water. Neither knew how to swim.

Pidge tried to put on his life jacket, but due to the extreme cold, his fingers could not tie the laces. Pidge was able to grab our father and haul him onto the capsized and upside down

vessel. Pidge did this three times in the estimated ninety minutes the two were in the water. This effort is what kept our father from drowning. The last John saw of Pidge he was clinging to an empty gas can for flotation as he slipped beneath the surface of the frigid water.

On March 8, 2013, Alvin "Pidge" Beal was posthumously awarded the United States Coast Guard Certificate of Valor by Senator Susan Collins. The day of the award would have been his 58th birthday.

Brown Eyed Girl

Craig Robinson
Corea

Named after my brown eyed wife Cheryl.

Maxine D and *Zachary J*

Steve Dow
Owls Head

I started lobstering in a 23-foot boat with a 5-horsepower Make-and-Break one-cylinder engine. We went into the woods and collected spruce to be bent for the bows in the traps that we made. My last two boats were the *Maxine D*, after my wife, and the *Zachary J*, after my great-grandson.

Amazing Grace

Doug Anderson
Port Clyde

After twenty years of scalloping and ground fishing, I decided to come home and go lobstering. So I pulled an old boat out of the woods that my grandfather had owned. It had been built for Victor Ames in 1948 at Rockland Boat Shop. The boat and I were the same age. I fiberglassed the hull and named it after my grandfather, Forest L. Davis, otherwise known as Ford Davis. I was afraid people would confuse the name with Ford automobiles, so I dropped the "r" and named it the *FOD*. The *FOD* is still operating today at age 65.

After a life changing spiritual encounter in 1993, I bought a boat from David Audio that had burned down to the deck. Wesley Lash brought it back to life and so, for the sake of my life changing experience and the boat having new life, I named it *Born Again*. Continuing with my theme of spiritual names, my next boat was the *Glory Bound.* My last and most beloved boat

AMAZING GRACE

PORT CLYDE

was the *Amazing Grace*. My grandson, Kyle Clough, owns and operates her now.

I've had many other boats: The *Miss Kirsty* , the *Miss Kirsty II*, and the *Rhonda Louise* were all named for loved ones.

All Set

Richard Albertson
Phippsburg

Back in 1998 I had Glen Holland build me a boat. This in all probability would be my last boat, having virtually retired from pushing pretty hard for most of my life.

I was taken with the often used expression, "all set," by folks when things were going reasonably well and most situations were pretty well in hand. Ergo, *All Set* became the boat's name.

Sea Mist

Darren Shute
Stockton Springs

I bought my boat from my father a few years ago, before he passed away from failing-health issues.

In 1997, my father had a new 36-foot Northern Bay boat built. In the fall it was delivered to his home so we could finish it off. It was situated some distance from the house, with Stockton Harbor in the background. We were working on it 16 to 18 hours a day and every day he would solicit ideas for a name from whomever dropped by.

One foggy morning, as we took a break for coffee and some of my mothers homemade blueberry muffins, we sat at the kitchen table as it started to mist, breaking the fog just enough so the boat appeared in sight with the harbor in the background.

My dad said, "I know what her name will be—*Sea Mist*." That's how it came to be.

Bodacious

James Knight
Harpswell

My boat, *Bodacious*, is a 38-foot Duffy hull, new in 2004. I have always liked the word bodacious. The dictionary says it is a Southern colloquialism, a blend of the words bold and audacious. The word had two things going for it: I had never seen it on a boat, and it describes my attitude toward the entire lobster industry. I love my job in every way—the sights, smells, and scenery. The physical things like open air, the equipment, working with my hands, and on and on and on.

Bigfoot & Carrisa

Jennifer Alley
Beals Island

Bigfoot and Carrisa are the names of my two poodles.

Bug Catcher

Gerry Cushman
Port Clyde

I am a fifth-generation fisherman from Port Clyde and purchased my boat in 1989. After weeks of deliberation, and at a friend's suggestion, I named her *Bug Catcher*, as fishermen often refer to lobsters as "bugs" when we're out on the water.

Sundown

Robert Cates
Cutler

I spent a lot of time with my father looking for herring at sundown.

Abbie Rose

Chris Anderson
Port Clyde

Abbie Rose is the name of my first-born daughter (the only one born at the time the boat was named). She was named after her two great grandmothers, who were huge influences in the lives of my wife and I. Abbie was the name of my wife's grandmother and Rose is the middle name of my grandmother.

My grandfather once had a boat named *Bena Rose*, so it also brings a feeling of nostalgia.

Ain't Much

Dennis Eaton
Deer Isle

When I was a scallop fisherman in the 1970s, I had a skiff that was about forty years old that I used as a tender. A former scalloper named Steve Robbins called me on the CB and said, "Your skiff ain't much and it has sunk."

That name stuck for my skiff. I fixed it up and I'm still using it today. In 2000 I found myself having a Peter Cass 36-footer built—real nice boat, but due to circumstances I could not control, I had to give it to my son.

I was unemployed and with too much salt in my veins—I could not stand that—so I went off to Swans Island to look at a 1964 wooden Jonesporter. Not a bad boat for someone my age. She gets me there and back. So what do I name it? Why not for it's age—like me, she *Ain't Much*.

Camando

Bob Ober
York Harbor

My boat's name is the *Camando*. I came up with the name by combining the names of my three children, Cady, Amanda, and Douglas. The photo is from my daughter Cady's wedding.

Newsboy

Alan Philbrook
Owls Head

I found the name *Newsboy* in a history of Owls Head, Maine. The book told of a very special clipper/bark schooner that was built right in Owls Head in the years 1855 thru 1865. It was built very close to where I now moor my lobster boat, also called *Newsboy*.

Chelsea Margaret

Erich S. Culver
Port Clyde

About five or six years ago my friend and summertime neighbor, John Sibley, was paddling his kayak around Port Clyde Harbor looking at all the lobster boat names. When he came ashore his statement to me was. "the Aristocracy name their boats after their wives and daughters and such. The rest are just Rebels."

I thought this was a great line and I have used it many times! By the way, my boat is named after my daughter and grandmother. They are the two most important people in my life.

Ol Griz

Herbert Huckins
Corea

My old boat used to be named after my wife. I told her she had her turn, now it was time for the dog's turn.

Griz was a cross between a Newfoundland and a sheepdog. As he got older I called him Ol' Griz.

Miss MJ

Joseph A. Pinkham
Georgetown

My 33-foot Crowley Beal lobster boat is named for my daughter Millicent and my wife Jillian, who support me one hundred percent in this up-and-down industry.

Hard Shel

Sheldon Pope
Biddeford Pool

My son, Sheldon Pope lobsters out of Biddeford Pool. His boat is named *Hard Shel*. He has been lobstering since he was fourteen. Since he didn't have a girlfriend at the time, and naming the boat after sisters or his mother didn't appeal to him, the boat was named after himself. Therefore, one "L" in Hard Shel.

— Rhonda Hallett Pope

Retired Daze

Eugene Smith
Beals Island

This is the boat I always wanted but never had in my younger days. Now I am semi-retired and the boat was available. We chose the word "Daze" instead of "Days" because retired people are kind of in a daze.

Gramp's Crew

Erick Smith, age 17
Mathew Smith, age 15
Carol Smith, age 13
Tyler Smith, age 10
Beals Island

Eugene Smith—owner of *Retired Days*—has four grandchildren that fish his old boat.

RETIRED DAZE

BEALS, ME.

Just Because and *Why Knot*

Keith Smith
Beals Island

I got a new boat in 1989, but I had to wait a long time to get it. So I named her the *Long Wait*.

In 1997, I was at the Libby Boat shop and they were building a 34-footer. They said I oughta buy her. I went home and mentioned it to my wife and she said, "Why not?" So I bought her and named her *Why Knot*.

In 2007, I was getting a little older and my boys said I should get a bigger boat so I could fish longer in the season more comfortably. I decided it was a good idea. One day my grandson asked me, "Why are you getting another new boat?" I said, "Just because." So that's what I named her.

Emily Jane

Luke Abell
Mount Desert

My name is Emily Jane Wright. I have recently had a lobster boat named after me. My partner, Luke Abell, after ten years a sternman, got his lobster license. The boat he bought was the same boat he worked on for ten years. He renamed it after me, *Emily Jane.* Luke and I have been together for eight years. It is very exciting to see my name on the back of a boat when I come in and out of the harbor. Probably our story is similar to many. I think, though, that having a boat named after you is quite romantic.

Seaducktress

Amber Tonry
Edgecomb

My husband and I built this boat eleven years ago. I learned all about fiber-glassing, gel coating, and much more. My husband picked out the name because "she is a beautiful boat, built by his beautiful wife." He passed away last summer, so now my son and I will be fishing from the *Seaducktress.*

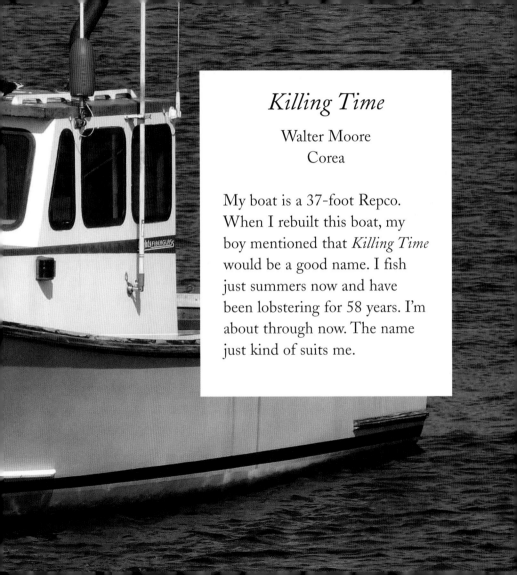

Killing Time

Walter Moore
Corea

My boat is a 37-foot Repco.
When I rebuilt this boat, my
boy mentioned that *Killing Time*
would be a good name. I fish
just summers now and have
been lobstering for 58 years. I'm
about through now. The name
just kind of suits me.

Mary Aline

Shawn Stanley
Bass Harbor

The *Mary Aline* is named for Shawn's wife, as many boats are. When he got divorced in 2009 he didn't want to go through the hassle and paperwork of changing the boat's name. So he crossed her out with a red line.

When we take the boat out of town and have it tied to a dock it's interesting to watch the confusion then the dawning of understanding on a man's face—usually a fisherman—when he reads the stern of the boat. The usual comment is, "well that's an original way to deal with the problem!" We're always surprised we haven't run into anyone else frustrated enough to have done this.

— Susan Dunbar, just the girlfriend.

Miss Peyton

Mark McGuire
Cutler

I am a little surprised that you need to ask the reason behind the name of my boat. After all it is named after the only little girl ever as far as I can tell.

All kidding aside, my boat is named after my granddaughter, Peyton Ella McGuire, and of course in Gramps' eyes she is the best little girl ever born. She is ten years old now and quite proud to tell people Gramps' boat is named after her. Peyton has her student license and her boat is named *Jarratt M.,* after her little brother.

Miss Behavin'

Trevor Jessiman
Cutler

If you want to know the truth, I'm kind of a hell raiser.

Mama And Magnum

Benita and Raymond Alley
Beals Island

I am Mama, Magnum is our dog.

Pier Pressure

Jason T. West
Steuben

The process of naming a boat is time consuming and much like naming a first child. It's a name you are stuck with for years to come, so you want it to be something meaningful.

Jason's boat name is *Pier Pressure* and it stems from the term for the social pressure by members of one's peer group to take a certain action, adopt certain values, or otherwise conform in order to be accepted. The majority of the other fishermen, in and around his bay, were building bigger boats. At the time, Jason had a 36-foot boat and the pressure was on for him to conform and build a bigger 40-foot boat, hence the name *Pier Pressure*.

—Jolette Rossi-West (spouse)

Pocket Change

Kerry McQuaid
Brunswick

Our boat name really goes back to when my dad used to work stern for my grandfather. His favorite saying to my dad was that lobstering was nothing but "easy money." The phrase stuck and now *Easy Money* is the name of my dad's boat.

I only lobster for recreation and fish out of a 16-foot skiff. In keeping with the tradition, I thought *Pocket Change* would fit nicely with *Easy Money,* because that's really all I make.

Number 7

Brian Marden
Harpswell

It's quite simple. *Number 7* is my seventh—and final—boat.

Pursuit

Kris Koerber
Owls Head

I have a pretty unique background in the lobster industry. I grew up in Brunswick, and at the age of seven began fishing out of a 15-foot flat-bottom skiff with my dad and older brother. Over the years I worked on various lobster boats in Harpswell through high school, college, and grad school.

After grad school, I moved to Owls Head, where I got on board the boat of the current president of the Maine Lobstermans Association. During this last year I have been preparing to take flight on my own. I bought a 22-foot South Shore in December 2012 and named her the *Pursuit.* I like the short, strong appeal of the name, *Pursuit*—an effort to secure or attain; a quest: the "Pursuit of Happiness."

Rebbie's Mistress

John Dourin
Cutler

My nickname is Rebby, from the song "Johnny Rebel." My boat, a 46-foot Wesmac, is my mistress. My wife wouldn't let me have a real one.

Stephanie G.

Wayne Lash
Friendship

My boat was named after my granddaughter, Stephanie Graylin Havener, and launched on her first birthday, August 12, 1977. Little Stephanie, with the help of her mother Pat, christened the boat with a bottle of ginger ale. I'm 83 and still fishing aboard the *Stephanie G.*

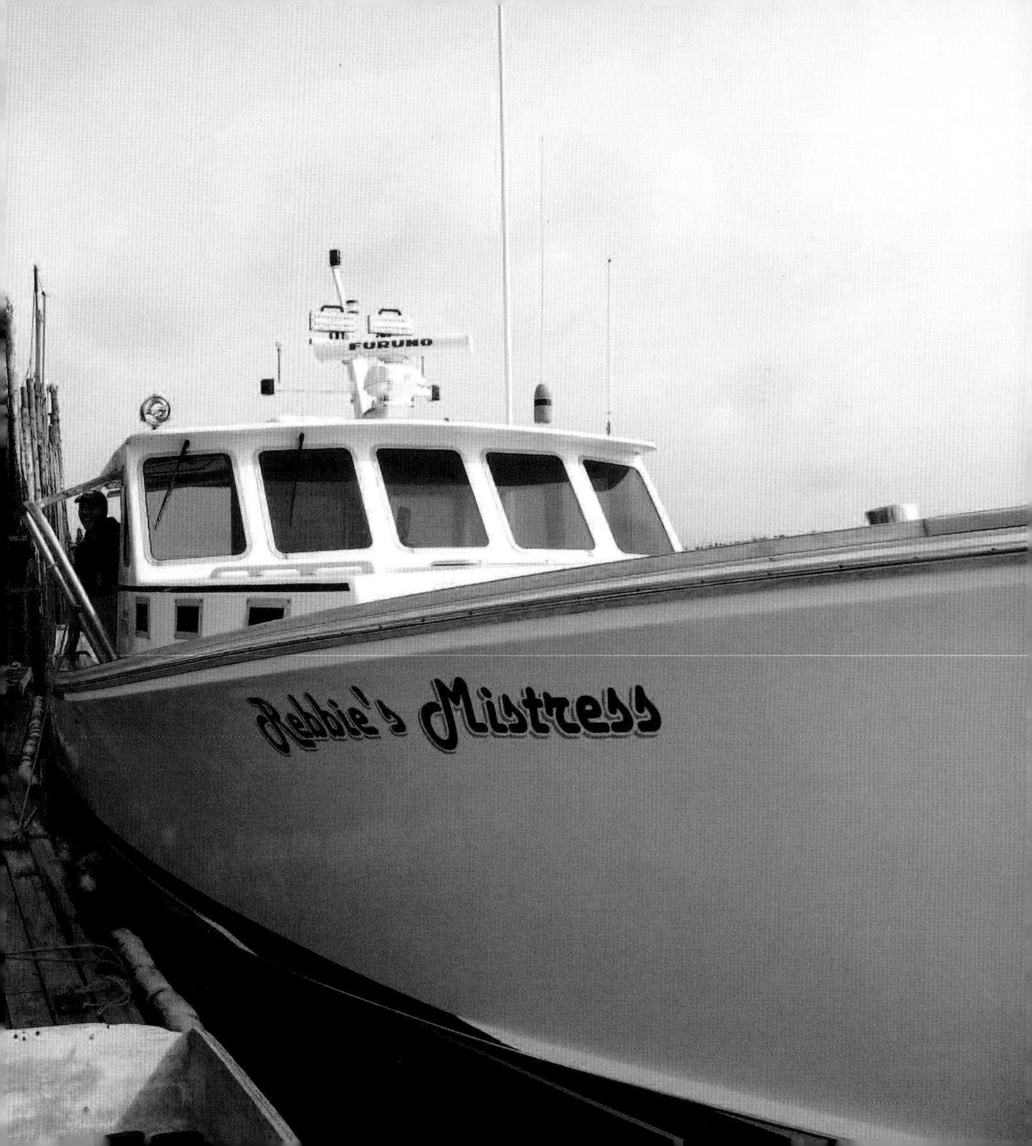
FURUNO
Mistress

Catch-22

Kasden Beal
Beals Island

This is the story of our son, Kasden Beal's 22-foot lobster boat, the *Catch-22*. He purchased this boat when he was 13 years old, in June 2010. The name was already on the boat and he liked it so well that after the boat was refurbished, he kept the name.

This is his first in-board lobster boat. He has been fishing since he was about 7, when I used to operate a small outboard boat to haul five traps with him. After that year, he obtained his own student license and his dad, Travis, fished with him by hand.

Travis spent much of the summer of 2010 fixing up the *Catch-22*, with some help from Kasden, my father, B. Willis Beal, and me pitching in here and there. The newly redone boat was launched at Beals in early July 2010, and Kasden fished the rest of the summer with it. He has continued to fish out of this boat since then during the summer and fall.

The name, *Catch-22*, stands for not only the boat's size (a fiberglass 22-foot Sisu) and its purpose of catching lobster, but is also a testament to both the benefits and the perils of the lobster business. While lobstering certainly can be a profitable business, there are many draw-backs to the industry, such as breakdowns, laws and limitations, high expense, and low price. However, Kasden enjoys fishing very much. It seems to be in his blood—his father Travis, his grandfathers Merle Beal and Willis Beal, his maternal great grandfathers Millard L Alley and Alfred Beal,his paternal great grandfather Clyde Peabody Sr., his paternal great-great grandfather Kenneth Beal, his maternal great-great grandfather Leon Alley, and so forth were all fishermen, so despite all the possible problems and setbacks, he chooses to pursue lobster fishing and the lifestyle it provides.

— Glenda Beal

Semper Paratus

Larry Smith
Roque Bluffs

The name of my vessel is *Semper Paratus*, which is Latin for "Aways Ready." The name was a suggestion from my daughter, in view of my having served thirty plus years in the United States Coast Guard. Since that is the Coast Guard's motto, she thought it would be a good fit. I tend to agree.

Lost Airmen

Andy Mays
Southwest Harbor

My boat is named in honor of my Uncle Bobby and his B-17 crew. His name was Louis Machovec and he was a ball turret gunner. On March 23, 1944, they were on their fifteenth mission—to attack German aircraft manufacturing factories in Brunswick, Germany. They were hit by flack over the target and fell out of formation. Their lone aircraft was an inviting target and they withstood an hour of fierce fighter attacks. Their pilot, 2nd Lieutenant Fletcher Johnson, radioed that many of his crew were seriously wounded; if he landed and surrendered, they would not survive. He was headed home to get them to the hospital.

Over the middle of the North Sea, James Stone, an American P-47 fighter pilot, observed the crippled B-17 jettisoning guns and equipment in a desperate attempt to stay in the air on one engine, but they ended up ditching. The fighter pilot

watched five of the ten-man crew exit the bomber before it sank. Two men made it into a life raft. Stone circled low and dropped his own raft to the others who were treading water. He radioed their position to the British Air/Sea Rescue Service, which had patrol boats along the designated return route, ready to rescue downed crews.

Running perilously low on gas, Stone had to leave the crew. On his way home, he passed over the British patrol boat and affirmed that they were on a direct course to the downed airmen. Shortly after, two more P-47 fighters returning to England saw what they believed was a German patrol boat. They strafed it and attacked it with rockets, setting it ablaze and killing ten of the thirteen British crewmen—and sealing the fate of the five Americans waiting to be rescued.

A second British boat picked up two of the patrol boat's crew, clinging to a piece of boat wreckage and holding the body of the eleventh man who died after the attack. They continued to the position of the downed B-17 but, after several hours of searching, were unable to locate any survivors.

Redneck Girls

Heather Thompson
Harrington

I come from a long line of fisherman, so throughout my life we have had many boats. I personally have owned three. My boat now was built in 2007. I named it *Redneck Girls* because I am the captain and I take my sister Hilary as sterngirl. We have been considered rednecks for most of our lives. We like to think that is a good thing. As women, we like to hunt and fish, we have fun doing things outdoors, *and* we work hard! We're both married and have kids who keep us busy—besides hauling our 800 traps.

Corea Choice

Ryan Bridges
Corea

I fished out of a small 20-foot skiff and outboard (*Rising Tide*) that I bought when I was
ten years old and fished out of until I graduat-
ed high school.

After graduating I bought my second
boat, a 35-foot Osmond Beal from an older
fisherman who had passed away, but who had
also fished out of Corea. It was my "career"
choice, so I used a play on words and came up
with *Corea Choice*.

At Last

Tyler R. Hodgon
Boothbay

My boat is named for the song sung by Etta James. That was our wedding song. We bought the boat, my wife changed jobs, and we got married all in the same week. That was a busy week. The boat was built as a spec boat in 1999—the year I bought it—and was originally named *Millennium*.

My previous boat was a wooden boat named *Tippecanoe*, from the popular campaign song and slogan of the Whig party in 1840—"Tippecanoe and Tyler Too."

Bad Behavior

Richard Smith
Beals Island

To tell you how I decided on this name, I have to tell you how I decided to name the boat I had before it, but it's not really that interesting a story.

My father was getting ready to paint the name on my previous boat, which I bought roughly seven years ago, and informed me that I had to decide on one for certain before he could put it on. Completely on a whim, and just for the fact that it would make people wonder, I decided to name it *Bad Intentions*. When the time came last year to name my current boat, I decided there was only one thing that could follow *Bad Intentions*—*Bad Behavior* seemed like the only way to go.

Endurance

Paula Jean Lunt
Tenants Harbor

The *Endurance* is a 32-foot Holland powered by a 210-horse-power Cummins diesel. It was finished by William S. Lunt and launched in November 2004. It is used for lobstering 800 traps.

It was originally named because I am an endurance athlete—marathons, distance paddling, triathlons, bike rides, etc. As someone who has grown up on the water and always gone lobstering, I found that it is good training for my athletic endurance events, and these events also make it possible to withstand endurance days lobstering, especially when hauling single handedly.

Though not the reason for my boat's name—but surely a nice coincidence—like me, Ernest Shackleton was born February 15, loved the sea, loved to explore, and captained a boat called *Endurance.*

Gramps Bird

Patrick Faulkingham
Winter Harbor

When my son named his daughter Robin Lynn, I told him I was going to call her Bird. She does not like being called Bird. but the boat name remains.

Michael Alan

Pat Hanley
Bass Harbor

Michael Alan is a 32-foot Mitchell Cove powerboat built in 2000. It was originally named *Audrey L,* after my now-ex-wife. In 2009, my 16-year-old nephew, Michael Alan Lewis, was killed in a traffic accident. Not long after, I decided to pay tribute to him by putting his name on my boat.

Divine Providence and *Bay Lady II*

Loren Faulkingham
Beals Island

Divine Providence was built in 2004 by Norman Libby of Jonesport. The origin of the name is the idea that all that we have is provided by God. This goes for the assurance of eternity in Heaven when this life is over, our daily health, all we have, all we are allowed to do. And it also has a special meaning due to the fact that we adopted our son in 2002. God had a plan in that, too. The symbol in the middle of the name is a sailor's crucifix, like the one my wife gave me for our first wedding anniversary.

I also have a second boat, *Bay Lady II,* that was finished by Ernest Libby, Jr. of Beals. It is a 35-foot Young Brothers and was just a sequel to my first outboard boat that was named *Bay Lady*, also built by Ernest Libby, Jr. No real story behind that, except that my dad heard the boat name on the CB one day and liked it, so we used it.

Barbara Ann

Bruce Fernald
Islesford

My first boat was named *Pa's Pride*. I bought the boat from my younger brother who had named it. I'm not sure if I lived up to the name or not.

My second boat was named *Stormy Gale*, after an old girlfriend, and was built three years before I got married. My third boat was named *Double Trouble*, after my twin sons—they were actually never any trouble, so the boat was misnamed.

My present boat is named after my wife, mother-in-law, wife's grandmother, and my aunt. They are all named Barbara Ann.

Becky's Worry

Wally Horton
Blue Hill

My little boat's name is *Becky's Worry* after my mother. This came to me a long time ago when both my brothers were in Vietnam and on my own I acted poorly and down right bad.

All of the rest of the family constantly said to me, "Damn it, Wallace, you worry your poor mother so." This was usually followed by all the ways I could do so much better.

I miss them all now that it's just my brothers and me. I wish all of them were still here so I could feed them lobsters and take care of them and, yes, worry about them.

Chill Factor

Rolf Winters
South Thomaston

My boat's name is *Chill Factor,* which I chose because of my last name.

Cool Change

Randy Eaton
Brooklin

Randy Eaton named his boat *Cool Change* because of the song "Cool Change" by the Little River Band. About six years ago he gave the Little River Band a ride on his boat!

— Liz Walker (telling this for Randy, who does not indulge in the computer)

Crabby

Parker Murphy
Bass Harbor

I am 14 years old and have been lobstering since I can remember. My first lobster boat was a little skiff that my dad fixed up for me so I could fish in the harbor using a couple of his lobster traps and tags because I wasn't old enough to have a student license yet.

My dad told me that boats were girls and I should name it after the most important girl to me. I named it *Crabby* for my mom because I thought she was crabby most of the time. When I was eight years old my dad built me a 20-foot lobster boat and he told me the same thing. I figured my mom still seemed crabbier than ever, so I named it the *Crabby II*.

My mom and dad were shopping in Bar Harbor a few summers back and saw a rowboat in one of the gift shops that the shop owners were using to display souvenirs. They pulled the truck right up on the sidewalk and carried the rowboat out, put it

in the truck and brought it home. My dad fixed it up because it was really old and leaked and gave it to me for a punt to get out to the *Crabby II* on the mooring.

One day I came home from school and my mom told me that she had named the punt, *The Slub*. She told me that a slub was a cross between a slob and a slug so I guess she paid me back for naming my boat *Crabby* after her.

Crystal Sea

Richard Carlson
Saint George

People may think this name represents the beautiful ocean water, but *Crystal Sea* is actually named after our two children, Crystal and Sean (dropped the "n").

Daywatcher

Richard Waldron
Spruce Head

I took the name from the title of a book, *The Daywatchers*, written and illustrated by Peter Parnall, a long-time friend of mine. It is a book about birds of prey from around the world—eagles, ospreys, hawks, falcons, and such.

Designer's Daughter

Travis Beal
Beals Island

Designer's Daughter was built by RP Boat in 1999, the first 40-footer designed by Willis Beal—the plug had been finished for another Beals Island fisherman, but ours was the first actually built from the mold.

Willis is my father, and since he designed the boat my husband was buying, we decided to name the boat *Designer's Daughter*, in reference to both me and my dad. The idea was my mother-in-law, Regina Beal's.

— Glenda Beal

Gimmie A Hulla

Yvonne Rosen
Vinalhaven

My grandmother's name is Priscilla and when she and her brother were young, he could not say her name, so he started calling her Hulla. I wanted to name it after her and I thought that *Gimmie A Hulla* instead of "Give Me a Holla" was pretty clever.

Hello Darlin

Genevieve Kurilec
Stonington

I chose this name for a number of reasons. First off, it's catchy and I like the way it sounds over the VHF radio: "Hello Darlin, you on this one?" My first name, Genevieve, can sometimes be a challenge.

Endangered Species

Brian Smith
Beals Island

I named my boat for the endangered species—not the lobster or the whales—but the men who fish for lobster. All the new government regulations have made fishing more difficult and dangerous.

Lynny Lizzy

Lynette Mitchell
Harpswell

I fish out of Ash Cove in Harpswell. I decided to go lobstering about twelve years ago after losing my job. I stem from generations of lobstermen, so it seemed the logical choice. Although several family members have lost their lives on the water, including a brother, I still love the ocean.

Lynny Lizzy was a nickname given to me by a very special lady who used to watch me as a little girl—short for Lynette Elizabeth.

My boat is unique and she keeps my head above water, so to speak. She is my best friend.

Empty Pockets

Brian Densmore
Gouldsboro

Brian said he named his boat because, "You are always fixing something that is broken, and your pockets are always empty." My Ford Explorer has the license plate, "EMT PKTS" and Brian's Ford F-350 has the license plate, "PKTS EMT."

— Karen Densmore

Katherine Rachel

Phillip Morris
Tenants Harbor

This is a short story about my boat name. Katherine is my mother's first name. She would be one hundred last May. Rachel is my mother's mother. I was six years old when she died in 1948, at age 63. I remember Rachel only because she made me jelly and peanut butter sandwiches.

Fifth Day

Joe Staples
Swans Island

My husband, Joe Staples, decided it was high time to have a new boat built with me in mind. I have been his stern "man" for what seems like eternity. In 2000 he went to Down East Boats & Composites in Penobscot for a discussion with the owner, John Hutchins. He liked the 36-foot hull, so the work began and I gave input on how the work area should be set up to make the boat handy for me.

The prior boat wasn't very user friendly for me and I often found myself in the dangerous position of having to stand in the rope as it was being fed out, which was a huge factor in his decision to have another boat built.

Progress was rapidly being made and we needed to come up with a name for the new boat. I'd had enough of boats being named after me, Belva Rae. It wasn't until after my name was emblazoned across the stern of the previous boat that I learned to my dismay that it had a wide stern. I always wondered if people made the connection, especially considering the fact that my husband mentioned it constantly.

Joe gave the name a lot of serious thought this time and kept coming up empty. He asked me for help but he nixed everything I came up with. One night, while taking a shower, he actually prayed about it—he does some of his best praying in there—and asked God what he should name his boat. The answer that immediately popped into his mind was, "Call it the *Fifth Day*."

My husband's first thoughts were: "What on earth does that mean?" "Why not the *Seventh Day*?" "What happened on the fifth day, anyway?"

It seemed as though God said, "Go look it up."

When he came into the living room he was unusually quiet and went directly to fetch the Bible. He opened it up to the "Genesis 1" account of creation and to his surprise, in verses 20 through 23, he read the following:

And God said, Let the waters bring forth abundantly the moving creatures that hath life, and the fowl that may fly above the earth in open firmament of heaven.

And God created great whales, and every living creature that moveth, which the waters brought forth abundantly, after their kind, and every winged fowl after his kind: and God saw that it was good.

And God blessed them saying, Be fruitful and multiply, and fill the waters in the seas, and let the fowl multiply in the earth.

And the evening and the morning were the fifth day.

Joe thought the *Fifth Day* made perfect sense because there was no way the boat could be called the *Seventh Day*. He'd have to work hard to pay for it and there would not be any real rest involved. God had made the abundance of the sea and it was his job to get out there and harvest it.

Joe showed me the Bible, looked at me, and said "The boat is going to be named the *Fifth Day*." After reading it, I replied, "*Fifth Day* it is."

Joe told me later on that if he'd known that God was going to answer his question so quickly, he would have asked for the winning Power Ball numbers, too. We've always believed in asking big, but messed up that time.

Oh yes, and just to clarify, the name *Fifth Day* does NOT imply that he needs to consume a fifth to get through each work day. I thought it wise to clear that up.

— Belva Rae

Sofie Dall

Aaron Lyman
Sedgwick

The name, *Sofie Dall,* is a combination of my wife's name, Lynnie Dall, and our daughter's name, Sofia. We call her Sofie.

Gull

Stanley E. King
Arrowsic

I've had the boat for eighteen or nineteen years. Before me, the previous owner, a local lobsterman and friend, had the boat a long time and it was called *Gull*.

When he bought the boat the name was *Gull* also. The boat is a 30-foot 1968 Repco in pretty good, if not very good, shape. The name is still *Gull* because neither of us dared to change the name, thinking it might give us bad luck.

The name has become very fitting, as most of the younger and better financed guys have bigger boats, the maximum number of maximum traps, and have taken over most of the fishing area. The *Gull* is left picking up the leftovers! At age 58 my outlook is bleak.

Jackpot and *Lil Jackpot*

Lily Gray
Brooksville

My name is Lily and I am working on my student lobster license. I am twelve years old and this is my second year. I have two boats. The first one is *Lil Jackpot* and the new one is *Jackpot*. I named them that because my little brother's name is Jack, and some people call lobster traps "pots," and it sounded cool.

Jarsulan 4

Brent Oliver
Deer Isle

The name of Brent Oliver's current boat is *Jarsulan 4.* "Jar" is for our son Jarvis. He died of leukemia at age 4. "Su" is for me, his wife, Susan Oliver. "Lan" is for our daughter, Hollan Oliver. The "4" represents the fourth Jarsulan. Four was also always my daughter's number in high school sports, so we kept it the number 4 rather than the roman numeral, IV.

Silver Dollar

Merle Beal
Beals Island

When we decided to have a boat built I told my husband Merle that I wanted the hull black, I did not want my name on the bow, and I wanted the cabin large enough to go camping with the three kids. One day I was thinking about the name and I asked Merle if he remembered the silver dollar his grandfather gave him when he was born; and the one his father gave him, and the one his father gave our son, Wayne?

I told him we had all three silver dollars and that way the boat would be named for four generations. Thus she was named *Silver Dollar*, and all three were built into the bulkhead. They are still there after 43 years.

— Regina Beal

Grampy's Toy

Travis Dennison
Cutler

This was my dad's boat. His name was Connor Dennison and it was named with the help of his grandchildren. It was his toy.

Essex

George Anderson
Scarborough

The name of my lobster boat, *Essex*, was the name of the aircraft carrier I served on in the '60s.

Emmy Lou

Teddy Mclaughlin
Port Clyde

My daughter's name is Emily Louise. Emily is a name her mother picked—why, I can't remember. Louise is after my mother, grandmother, and my sister, who all are Louises. We're also huge Emmy Lou Harris fans, so Emily Louise became Emmy Lou.

Gracie

Ed Glover
Owls Head

My boat *Gracie* is a 1979 wood Calvin Beal Jr. It is named after my mother, Grace. She was an Army Nurse in World War II. She served in England, France, and Germany with the 120th Station Hospital. There was more than one Willys Jeep in Europe that had the same name as my boat.

E-Z Rider II

Aaron Smith
Beals Island

My boat's name describes her pretty well; she is a big, comfortable, and seaworthy boat.

Boon

Coleman F. Smith
York

My lobster boat is named for Boon Island. My father was lighthouse keeper Hoyt P. Smith and I lived in lighthouses for fifteen years. Boon Island was the last lighthouse that I lived on (1935–1939), and we were the last family to live at that lighthouse.

Devocean

Jerry Potter
Gouldsboro

My boat is a 43-foot Lowell, built new in 2006. My wife looked up boat names on the internet and we decided this just about sums up my life of fishing on the ocean.

I started when I was ten years old in a skiff with an outboard and a few traps. As the years went on, I eventually got a bigger boat and have had a few more boats over the years. My life's work has been devoted to lobstering, as well as harvesting others things from the sea, such as sea cucumbers, urchins, and shrimp.

I am now 67 years old and I only fish for lobsters and haul my boat out during the winter months—I enjoy this time doing some coyote hunting.

This boat name pretty much sums up my devotion to the ocean and how God has blessed me with a job that I have enjoyed for so many years.

Falling Star

George D. Cushing
Whitefield

Falling Star was built in 1980 and I am still fishing from her. I am a fourth-generation lobster fisherman. My dad's boat name was *Scrimshaw*, but that is another story.

The *Falling Star* name was derived when I was seven or eight years old and riding to Portland with my parents to do some Christmas shopping. From the back of my parents' '56 Ford, I saw a bright falling star on that clear December night. It was the first falling star I had ever seen.

I asked my parents if they had seen it. My mother said, "Make a wish, but don't tell anyone what it is, and it will come true!"

So I made my wish and it came true—hence the name of my boat. And my wish upon that falling star is still coming true.

Fishing with Annette and *Fishin Chix*

Jack and Annette Potter
Gouldsboro

My husband, Jack and I both own lobster boats and we both have unique names for our boats. We bought Jack's boat more than ten years ago when we were fishing together on the same boat. We named it *Fishing with Annette* and there's a large fish net hanging off the corners of my name.

Then a few years ago I decided to go off on my own. I named my boat *Fishin Chix* and I have a happy lobster on each side of the name with pink bows on their heads. The lettering is all in pink as well. I named it this because small lobsters are called chix and so are women! I fish with a stern(woman), so I thought an all-girls boat needed a girly name. We are fishin' chix in every sense!

Islander

George Foye
Eliot

My family has fished from Cedar Island in the Isles of Shoals—six miles out from Kittery—for five generations. I was the last one to live on the island and lobster from it spring, summer, and fall. There was no electricity or running water. Everything had to be hauled up to the house by hand. As the other fishermen left the island for good, I was left alone.

As I got older it became harder and harder to get supplies up to the island at low tide. I left the island eight years ago, but still lobster there—I go back to town at night now.

I named my boat *Islander* because I spent my whole life out there, and in my mind I'm still there.

Katahdin Rose

James Long
Georgetown

My boat is named after my daughter. I don't know why we named her after a mountain, she's just a peanut. My dad's boat was named after my mother. It was the *Jane Carol*, and at that time there was another boat in the same harbor named the *Carol Jane*.

Shaina Mariah

Ronald Dennis
Hampden

Our story is pretty straightforward. We named our boat the *Shaina Mariah* after our two daughters, with a touch of the name *Santa Maria* singing in our heads.

Shitpoke

Amby Alley
Vinalhaven

When Amby was growing up he was quite tall and very skinny. When we married, he was 6'4" and weighed 165 soaking wet— skinny! His friends called him "Shitpoke" because he resembled a great blue heron, a tall bird with really skinny legs. They also called him "Big Bird!"

When Amby was fifteen, he bought his first boat, the *Daisy*, from Ronnie Shephard in Stonington. Over time, however, the name had completely worn off. One night, a group of his friends rowed out and put the name *Shitpoke* on the stern of the boat with black electrical tape and it stuck there until he sold the boat a couple of years later.

Amby went into seining, and when it became "big business," he got back into lobstering and sold his seining business. He immediately knew what he would name the new lobster boat—it just had to be the *Shitpoke*. Some have given him grief for the

name, but they don't know the history behind it. The Coast Guard calls the boat the "SS Poke."

It's quite funny that we now own a home in southwest Florida with a lot of great blue herons in the area. There's one that regularly visits our yard, especially when Amby is fishing in the canal. He wants Amby's bait!

— Pam Alley

Island Girl

Eliot Nixon
Brunswick

I fish part of Cohog Bay from Snow Island to Ragged Island. I chose *Island Girl* just because I liked it.

Rip Tide

Paul Rackliff
Wheelers Bay

My father's nickname was Rip. He got this by having a hard time waking up to go to haul, like Rip Van Winkle. At the age of 92, he was the oldest active lobsterman in the state. He quit lobstering, then died six months later. His boat was named *Mustang*, named the year Ford first introduced the Mustang car. I wanted to honor him by naming my boat *Rip Tide*.

Fire Storm

Ron Pendleton
New Harbor

After being a member of the Bristol Fire Department since 1954 (fire chief for 20 years, assistant chief for 25 years), I bought a lobster boat to do a little fishing in my retirement. I wanted to express my long-time fire career in the name, so I called it *Fire Storm*.

Chasin' Crustaceans

Dillan Cushman
Port Clyde

When I was younger and taking friends out to haul they would say, "Look at those crustaceans!" That's what lobsters are, and that name just stuck with me. So when it came time to name my boat, *Chasin' Crustaceans* worked. It's what I do.

Dark N' Stormy

Jack Thomas
South Freeport

My family has a history of playing games with boat names that have more than one meaning or interpretation. Past boat names have been *Tangent* (when I switched from sail to power boats), *Blackjack* (black boat), *Yard Sale* (a water-skiing boat). *Dark N' Stormy* goes back some thirty years to when my wife and I got married and honeymooned in Bermuda.

During our stay we enjoyed a few drinks of Goslings Black Seal Rum and Barretts Ginger Beer—also known as a "dark and stormy." As fate would have it, our stay in Bermuda was cut short because of a hurricane. My kids are now young adults and remembered our honeymoon story, so when I wanted to name the boat *Black Seal*, they quickly changed it to *Dark N' Stormy*. My older clients love the name as they think it must come from a novel about the sea.

Huron

Matthew Huron
York

I am a 21-year-old deaf lobsterman with a cochlear implant. The name of my boat is also my last name—Huron.

Starting Over

James Smith
Jonesport Beals

After I got divorced I felt like I was starting over.

Frederick E

Tim Butler
Seal Cove

My boat is named after my father, Frederick "Bubba" Butler. He fished out of the same harbor, Seal Cove, for many years. He was born in Seal Cove and served in World War II and was wounded with a serious head wound, leaving him blind in one eye and deaf in one ear. It never interfered with his lobster fishing, though. He died in my arms on the beach in Seal Cove at the age of eighty.

Ole Shoe

Alvin S. McNeilly
Owls Head

My wife Jennie B. McNeilly, now deceased, used this phrase often when talking to a family member or a dear friend. This term continues to be used in our clan in a loveable and meaningful manner.

Miss Piggy

Albert Buswell
Swans Island

I have lobstered at Swans Island all my life on a part-time basis. I am a retired teacher and still lobstering.

When my five children were small, our favorite TV show was *The Muppet Show*. When Miss Piggy made her appearance, I would "ooh" and "aah," much to my children's delight.

When I moved up from a small skiff, hauling by hand, to a 17-foot craft with a hauler, it was only natural that she receive that name—not to mention the stench that emanates by late August!

Daily Bread

Dana Tracy
Prospect Harbor

I have been fishing for forty years or so. My first couple of boats were named *Peggy Ann,* after my wife.

After we had children and I worked my way up to a new boat, I named it *Two Sons,* for obvious reasons. As my boys grew up and I decided to have one more boat, I thought about a new name that would sum up my career and what years I may have left to fish.

Being a man of faith, I was reading a devotional called "Our Daily Bread" and thought—that's it! The name of my new boat will be *Daily Bread.* That would sum up my thankfulness for how I have managed a living from the sea with my faith put first.

Ruthless

Justin Thompson
Port Clyde

I named my boat *Ruthless* because the day I got it my wife left me. I named my new boat after my soon to be ex-wife. Her name was Ruth, so I am less Ruth.

Taylor C

Ethan Fink
Round Pond

Taylor Catherine is our daughter's name, so we shortened it up for the boat to the *Taylor C*. She is named after her nana, my mother. I loved her dearly.

Pretty Woman

Nick Martinez
Orr's Island

Pretty Woman is a 36-foot Calvin Beal named after all the women in my life that have meant something to me. Also, a boat or a ship is always a she and I believe she is a pretty good looking lobster boat.

Sweet Freedom

Brian Alley
Beals Island

I love my freedom and we're losing it everyday.

Size Matters

Dixon Smith
Beals Island

My boat is a 41-foot Libby with a 750-horsepower Eveco engine. I didn't take the usual route of moving up gradually in the size of my boats. I went from a 28- to a 41-footer. Also, I'm a big guy and my family members are all big guys—people can think what they want.

Star Fisher

Steve Rosen
Vinalhaven, Maine

My boat's name is a combination of my kids' names. My daughter's middle name is Astrid, which means "Star." My son's middle name is Fisher.

Phantom

Nick Lemeiux
Cutler

My boat is a 47-foot H & H, stretched to 50 feet, and is powered by a 1000-horsepower Caterpillar engine. Here one minute and gone the next . . . she's elusive.

Jerry Rig

Jerry Grondin
Falmouth

My name is Jerry, and the term "Jerry Rig" refers to something put together with wire or whatever you have around. That's why my boat floats—it's Jerry Rigged.

My wife came up with this brilliant name. She was also not a fan of having this boat, or any boat, named after her.

There are more than 6,000 registered lobster boats in the state of Maine. We didn't hear from every one with their story, nor could we hope to fit them all into the book. We'll have another book, with the stories we couldn't include here, plus lots more. In the meantime, here are a few interesting sounding names whose meanings we'll leave to your imagination.

Beth Said Yes!	Shameless	Pimp My Barge
No Name	Scraps	The Other Woman
Crustacean Frustration	Catch-Em-All	Rotten Hog
Whiskey Girl	Aquadesiac	Uncle's UFO
Naughty Girl	What For	Addiction
Six Grand	Breakin Wind	Sugar Foot
Whatever	Thy Neighbor	Starlight Express
Aces High	Bip-Bop	Monster
Provider	Little Ugly	The Peanut
Touch of Madness	Wooden Shoe	High Hopes Isaiah
Indecision	Always Something	Bite Me
Outcast	Six Corkers	Never Rest
Uncle's Angels	Orny Grubbah	Frayed Knot
Under Pressure	Lobsta Mobsta	Keep Dreamin
Money Pit	Bad Obsession	250 Yards
Commode	Reef Creeper	Liquid Courage
Last Straw	Hard To Tell	Still Waiting
Money Shot	Miss Badonkadonk	Why Bother
Back Up Plan	I've Been Thinking	Stink Bomb
Hide and Seek	Nobody's Fool	Last Penny